WIRE WRAP JEWEL

GW00993565

The Complete Guide to making amazing wire wrapped pendants, earrings, rings and bracelets; everything you need to become a wire wrap jewelry pro

Jane Donald

copyright@2020

Table of contents

CHAPTER ONE

INTRODUCTION TO WIRE WRAP JEWELRY

Wire wrapping can simply be defined as taking wire and folding it over itself or beads as well as different mechanisms to produce gems or jewelries.

Wire wrapping is a skill that anyone can learn with determination and become a pro in making jewelries. The beautiful thing about creating wire wrapped gems or jewelries is that there is no particular method of going about it – you can make free shape designs with your wire, so making wire wrapped earrings is a fantastic path for tenderfoots to begin.

Wire wrapping can be utilized to produce a loop for combining various parts, for example, while making a wrapped wire circle or wrapping a pendant. Through wire wrapping, you can likewise tie down beads to a structure, or even connect non bead things, for example, wire wrapping rhinestone cup chain onto a bangle. At the point when wrapped, bended, bowed and controlled, the wire itself can turn into the structure and establishment of your piece or go about as a design detail. Wire wrapping lets you make custom shapes and edges, and gives you more approaches to utilize various parts together.

Wire wrapping is a skill that anyone can learn with determination and become a pro in making jewelries. The beautiful thing about creating wire wrapped gems or jewelries is that there is no particular method of going about it – you can make free shape designs with your wire, so making wire wrapped earrings is a fantastic path for novices to begin.

This book will show you how to make your own wire wrapped pendants, earrings and bracelets decently without facing any problem. It will require some training, yet it's truly fun on the off chance that you get the hang of it and it just takes a couple of moments.

CHAPTER TWO

HOW TO CARRY OUT WIRE WRAPPING FOR JEWELRY MAKING

The most ideal approach to learn wire wrapping is to see instructional exercises and adhere to guidelines from those effectively acquainted with this adornments making procedure. It tends to be hard to attempt to make sense of it all alone on the grounds that variables, for example, wire measure (thickness) and wire hardness can incredibly impact your outcomes. Attempting to achieve a design with an inappropriate sort of wire will make the task significantly more troublesome and can prompt disappointment, harmed fingers and terrible outcomes. Having the correct instruments, for example, forceps and cutters, will likewise help immensely.

To develop your wire wrapping techniques and skills, start basic with the very fundamentals, for example, making straightforward and wrapped wire circles or loops. Proceed onward to wrapping a briolette and making a herringbone wrap. The more you practice, the better your outcomes will be as you get acquainted with how wire acts and move. After you have aced a portion of the more basic methods, attempt wire wrapping beads onto a structure, making an over-under bushel weave plan and wire netting From here you can advance onto progressed procedures, for example, those exhibited by visitor fashioner Wyatt White. You can also check youtube for additional video guides and also practice and keep practicing to get better with wire bead jewelry making.

CHAPTER THREE

STAGES FOR CREATING WIRE WRAP JEWELRY PENDANTS

Stage 1: Materials

I like to utilize sea glass, and my clients like it as well, however you can truly utilize anything you need to wear, so be innovative.

Concerning wire, I utilize 18 gauge craft wire from BeadSmith that I simply request off Amazon, Silver, Brass, and Copper. Nonetheless, I strongly suggest you purchase a little roll of plain wire at your neighborhood tool shop to rehearse with before you get the real wire, in spite of the fact that it isn't so costly.

At the point when I previously began, the main devices I had were those red-took care of wire cutters appeared here, and a coordinating pair of needle-nose pincers. I immediately found these other, wondrous apparatuses known as level nose forceps, nylon-jaw pincers, and round-nose pincers. In the event that you are not comfortable, the nylon ones with the dark handles is for fixing utilized and bowed wire; it's extremely helpful, and I will show the other two.

The string I use is 1.5mm dark waxed cotton, from Shipwreck Beads, yet you can discover it on Amazon and different spots.

Stage 2: Getting Prepared

When you have your devices,
wire, and item(s) to be wrapped,
you have to choose precisely how
you need it to look. I for the most
part prefer to utilize a 'huge' back
piece, with a 'little' or 'medium'
piece on its facade, or a few little
pieces. Don't hesitate to utilize

anything you desire; I sometimes
use shells also, both as support
and little front pieces.

The more glass you have, the
better, so you can explore
different avenues regarding the
shadings to perceive what you
like the best. As I would see it,
practically any blue piece will look
great on a white piece, expecting
the sizes are acceptable.

Additionally, you need to figure
out which color of wire to utilize.
They all handle about the same
thing; however try different
things with the shades of the
glass to perceive what you need.

I utilize silver around 65-75% of the time since I like it the most.

So after you choose what you will wrap and with which tone, you have to remove the perfect sum. At the point when I decide the amount to utilize, I generally overlap the wire. The one I made for this guide was around 7" folder over, so 14". The two appeared here that have three pieces on them may get up to 9" folded. Despite the fact that, it won't damage to utilize an additional wire than you presumably need from the outset, since it truly sucks when you end up with insufficient to complete it.

Stage 3: The Loop

On to the wrapping! I realize they make unique circle making forceps with various sizes and everything, except hell, a pencil works totally consummately.

Simply take the wire and put up to the pencil at the pretty much community, and fold over twice. Presently, when the different sides return to be contorted together like appeared here, ensure they remain straight as though you planned to fold them over additional, the wires will need to traverse rashly. At that point, simply contort them more than once so the circle holds. I realized this may appear to be excessively confounding, and since the circle is such a significant part, I took a couple of additional photos to explain.

Stage 4: Kicking Off

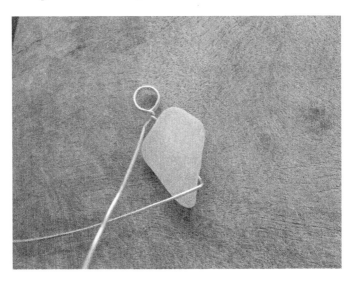

To begin, you will need to take the focal point off first until you can get some wire around only the back piece. I for the most part start one wire going on the back, and one on the front. For non-disarray, we should make the unfurled wire #1, and the one behind the glass that is collapsed, #2. Simply duplicate what I have done here and place the wire where you need it, and overlay one wire behind it.

Stage 5: The Wrapping

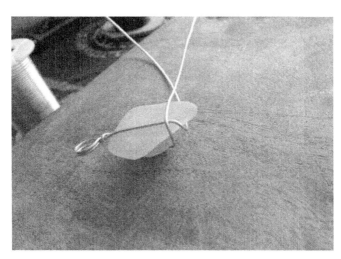

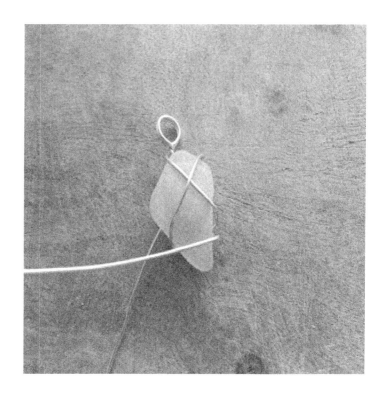

What I have done next is taken
#2 and just collapsed it over the
lower part of the white glass
piece.

Next, I took wire #1 and collapsed it corner to corner down-directly over the pink glass that I had recently positioned there, and afterward collapsed it around the back.

This is the part that may take some training. You need to ensure that you crease it as it were so it won't slip, and it must be 'tight'. You need to press solidly on the wire so it turns and adjusts to the shape as close as you can get it.

Next, I left #2, yet I took #1 and wrapped across slantingly the other way, and afterward back around the back.

From that point forward, I took wire #2 and took it back to the circle and folded it over once just to hold it. Thus, the main thing that #2 did was go down on the back, circumvent the base tip, and back up to the top, while #1 went down over, finished, up over, down over, at that point to the circle or loop.

I'm certain every one of that was excessively perplexing, yet it's exactly how I do it. I urge everybody to simply make what works, and from that point attempt and make something that looks great.

Stage 6: Completing the Process

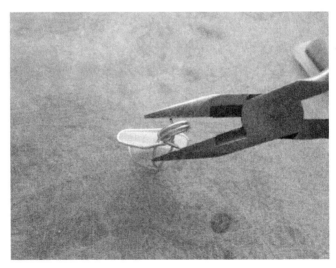

After you get the two wires back to the circle and folded over a couple of times, you have to shape or trim the wires, normally. Slice them to the length so the closures will wind up on the rear of the circle.

At that point, you have to mash down the end(s). This is the place the level nosed pincers or pliers come in. You take them, and simply squeeze the wire down, while pivoting the pincers around the base of the circle or loop.

You should now have a pendant that is almost complete

Stage 7: Adjusting and Tightening

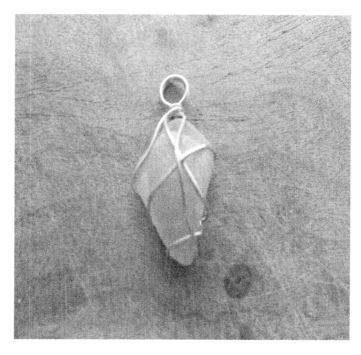

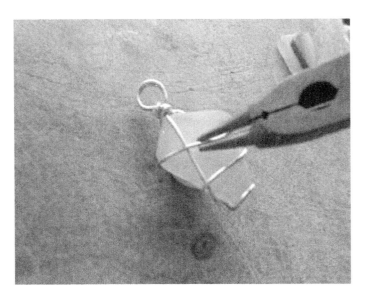

The exact opposite activity is
straighten out your masterpiece
to ensure it is useful and will keep
going quite a while, and shield
the glass from wiggling around in
the wire. I accept this is called
pleating, and this is the place the

round-nose forceps or pliers come in. Different forceps can be utilized, however they may harm or destroy the wire.

I by and large do this on the backs of the pendants, out of sight many at times.

Spot the tips of the forceps around a segment of wire, hold it immovably, and twist until you truly can't any longer. Be cautious now, on the grounds that any folds of wire that are not steady may slip and interfere with your workmanship. Simply pleat whatever you think, until you're sure that nothing will move around while it's being worn.

This is additionally an opportunity to make some other changes, such as adjusting the wires in the middle or so they cross uniformly.

Stage 8: Further Examples

This is simply one more model pendant that I figured out how to wrap nearly precisely the same way. I sort of the like it when 3 or so wires cross in the middle, I think it looks cool.

Stage 9: String and Wear or Give

I trust this was simple enough to follow and that it rouses a few people to go get a stone or some glass and wear it. I appreciate making these, since it's fun and simple, and I sell them.

I don't care to have pendants loose on the string, so, this is the reason I make them look ahead. I then simply circle the string through it and tie it off as a flexible necklace. By the way, these make extraordinary gifts.

Special thanks to you for taking your time to read it, I trust you loved it.

Stage 10: Further Examples

These are some others I took
time to make and I put them up
for sale. I trust this gives extra
motivation.

CHAPTER FOUR

GUIDELINES TO MAKE WIRE WRAPPED EARRINGS

The following are the basic tools and supplies you will need;

- Silver wire (0.8mm)

- Glass dots (your decision!)

- Earring hooks

- Jump rings

- Wire cutters

- Round nose pincers

- Snipe nose pincers

- Needle file (discretionary)

Stage 1: Preparing your wire for jewelry making

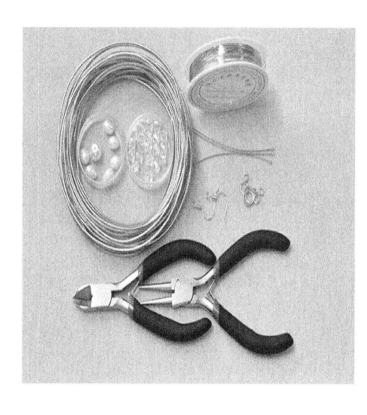

For this wire wrapped earrings
guide, I had suggest taking your
0.8mm wire and slicing it to a
length of roughly 24mm.

The length of your wire may likewise change contingent upon the size of your stones.

On the off chance that the beads you're utilizing are tiny, you may find that you have a great deal of surplus wire, however don't stress.

Additionally, as you practice this wire-wrapping strategy, as time goes on you'll have the ability to check better the measure of wire you need per stone.

Stage 2: Thread your beads and begin wrapping!

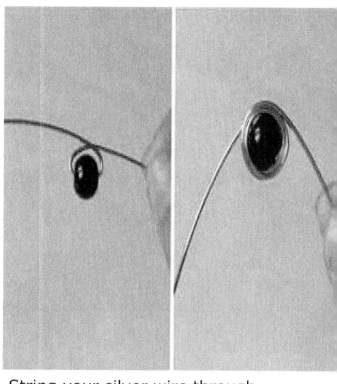

String your silver wire through the gap in your picked beads, ensuring that you leave some additional wire (approx. 50mm) jabbing or poking out of the head of your dot to join your ear hook later on.

Presently take the length of the wire at the lower part of the beads and begin wrapping.

With the primary wrap, ensure you wrap as firmly as could reasonably be expected.

To keep the bead safely set up, take your first wire wrap back up toward the head of the globule, where the short bit of wire is shooting out.

Presently envelop the wire by a downwards movement, again very close in position to the head of the bead, wrapping firmly as you go.

At that point presently you've protected the stone with your first wrap, you can get somewhat more innovative.

Proceed with the wrap the adornments making wire toward any path you like.

Follow the bend of the stone or make sharp mathematical examples – the decision is yours!

Stage 3: complete your wire wrapping neatly

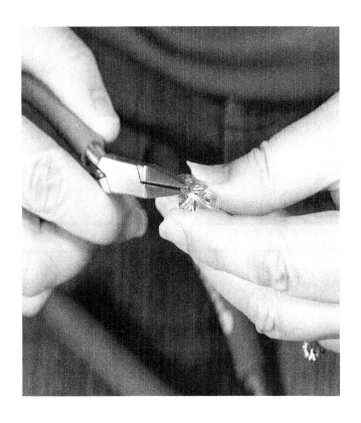

Glad with the example you've made with your wire wrapped earrings?

When you've wrapped the wire back to the head of the bead

where the head of the wire is standing out, you would now be able to start to clean things up.

Take the finish of the wire and start firmly folding it over the base of the wire that is at the head of the beads.

How frequently you wrap the wire is completely up to you – we'd suggest wrapping it in any event multiple times for a slick, and perfect completion.

You may likewise find that getting a tight wrap at this stage is somewhat dubious. Utilize your kill nose pincers to get a decent hold on the wire and to pull it tight as you wrap.

Tip: Remember that as you wrap the wire, there might be little holes between each wrap.

You can clean this up by taking your kill nose forceps and delicately pressing the circles together.

This will unite the circles and leave you with a significantly more expert look to your handcrafted wire wrapped studs.

Stage 4: Cut and neaten your gems or jewelry wire

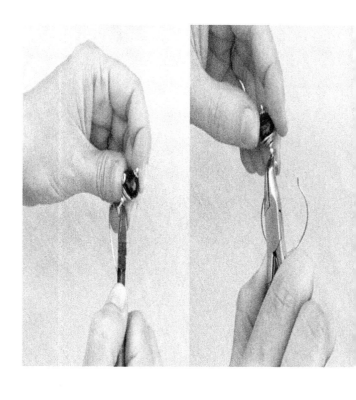

When you're glad and satisfied with the position and look of the three circles that are folded over the base of the top bit of wire, you can cut the surplus wire off with your wire cutters.

On the off chance that there are little burrs, you might need to run a needle document along the edge of the slice to eliminate any sharp edges.

You would then be able to fold the finish of the wire away underneath one of the current circles so it's protected.

From that point forward, return and neaten the circles with your kill nose pincers if necessary.

Stage 5: Create a little circle at the base of the wire

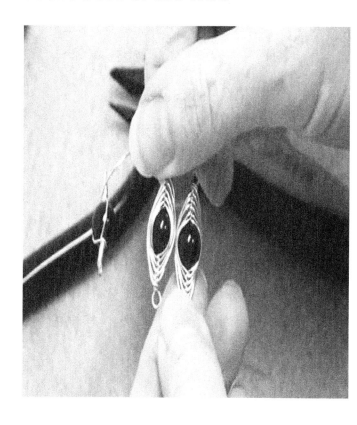

Simply over those three circles you've made, you would now be able to make a little circle.

This will hold your stud or earring hook, so it's significant that this is secure and has no holes for your jump ring or hoop snare to come free.

Utilizing the finish of your round nose pincers, enclose the wire by a total circle, and push the surplus aside.

Ensuring you have a total circle, take your wire cutters, and cut the surplus wire.

Likewise, as referenced above, in the event that you have any sharp burrs or edges where you've cut the wire, run a needle file over the outside of the finish of the wire in order to ensure that no sharp edges is seen.

Stage 6: Add your earrings discoveries

Presently you've made the fundamental aspect of your wire wrapped earrings with these 6 Easy Steps to Make Wire Wrapped Earrings; you can complete the plan with a hop ring and a stud hook of your decision.

And you should simply open your jump ring utilizing your snip nose forceps or pliers.

Printed in Great Britain
by Amazon